I0546104

THE
SPOKEN WORD
POETRY

CORA GEORGE

This Book is Dedicated

To

My beautiful daughter Lashana George

Table of Contents

APPRECIATION

I like to thank my Savior Jesus Christ. Thanks to my husband Johnnie George Sr., my daughter Krystal, my brother Walter and his wife Genise Brim, they made this book possible. Thanks to Arlena Shepard Thomas who ask the question, "Cora what are you doing?" "I said writing a book" (we both laugh). I also like to thank the host of my family and friends, you know who you are.

YOU AND I CAN MAKE A DIFFERENCE

You and I can make a difference in somebody's life.

I have believed God is ready to use you today.

God is a sweet, wonderful, kind, awesome, and famous God.

He is above all names and all Gods.

He can turn our dark world into beautiful light.

He can make the strange into something real and right.

He can take a nobody and make them a somebody.

He can take ugly and make it beautiful.

He can make someone who cares only for "self" care for everyone.

He can make you want to make a difference in someone's life.

You will want to be helpful instead of being selfish.

He will make you give rather than always wanting to receive.

He can make someone who can't write a good sentence into a poet.

He can make someone who had no ambition into someone eager to learn.

He can make someone who can sing into a singing star.

He can make someone who always walking buy a car.

He can make someone who wants to give up life be motivated to live again.

Let your life make a difference in this world.

MOTIVATION

Getting to the top.

No time to stop.

Have to go can't say no.

Must run to the end.

If I lighten up I won't gain.

Must motivate yourself because the rotten cards were dealt.

We have to keep on striving while others are sitting around jiving.

No money in the bank, don't worry one day you will, don't wait on anybody.

Need to keep on pushing.

Stand up and fight, stop sitting on your cushion.

BEING FAITHFUL

The work of the Lord requires Being faithful. The ministry that God gives you is what He expects you to carry out. He has all different types of ministries. But you must be bold in your calling. The work of the Lord is to be very important. Not bring home half-heartedly. The more you work the more He rewards you. He wants you to be faithful until death. Many claims to be a preacher and do not do what God requires. They will not say what God says. They compromise the gospel. So we all must stop and look at ourselves and get our ministries up to par. The Lord is looking at us. He wants willing vessels and not cowards. He wants soldiers in His army to fight. He can't use the ones who do not want to be strong and courageous. The Lord's army is special it is significant. It has a meaning it has a purpose. The more work you do the more results will come that are important. Don't be a spectator or someone pushing in the wrong direction. But use your energy and resources to save souls and to lift the hopeless, the homeless, the careless, and the unconcerned to pull them out of the darkness. Our commandments are to go into all the nations and teach all men the gospel. So why don't we have positive results? Because we are not performing the Great Commission that God has put before us. When souls are lost look at what you can do to prevent one soul from being burned in hell. Stop faking your way and pray your way. Stop being idle and be useful. Be a giver and not a taker. Be a winner and not a quitter. Be a helper and not a hinder. Be strong and not weak. Be positive and not negative. Don't give up and don't give out. Don't stop working for the Lord don't quit. Evangelism is our business.

STEP UP LOOK OUT AND TAKE A STAND

Step up and look out at your society today. Stop burying your head in the sand. Too many times we all want to casually go on about our everyday lives and do nothing about our world, better yet our society.

Our young are taking each other out daily. Everyone seems to take it so lightly. Our old are afraid to stay at home or answer their doors. They are afraid to go to the store. You care or you don't care. You speak out or you don't. It is our choice why not band together and save lives. You know it could be our own lives we are saving. Stop saying that's a shame. I think it's a shame for us to keep going merrily by and sit on our hands and do nothing. We close our ears so we can't hear. We shut our lips and say nothing. It's time now to band together and take a stand. How many useless crimes do you want to see happen?

Step Up Look Out and Take A Stand!!

MOVING ON

Time has come and gone now it is time to move on.

The past was cruel, but the future is victorious.

Some say there is no escape, but God has given us great VICTORY!

Our eyes are dim with yesterday's dreams. Today is drawing nigh. Our hearts are prepared with great expectancy. Our hopes are borrowed from the sky.

We seek to love.

We seek to care

We need wisdom and peace not despair

Our future has moved to another home.

A SPECIAL TRIBUTE TO MY MOTHER

It's not a loss it is a gain a beautiful win beneath earth very plain.

Carefully chosen and given to me, my mother

There's no other place she'd rather be.

He spoke to me with a great deep voice. I knew what it was He said.

The word was this, I'm not dead. A smile with gentle tears upon his face telling me I love you as we embrace.

Can't stop now got to go. Heaven awaits me at my post.

The love from momma is so dear, only she knows how to hollow a cheer.

She gave care and God is available to watch her at His table.

God is love He loves you. Written with a special and undying love for my mother.

YESTERDAYS DREAMS

Yesterday's dreams were never fulfilled.

Yesterday's dreams are never lived.

Tomorrow is too late.

Today won't wait.

Yesterday's dreams have already gone by.

Oh, how I hoped and dreamed of a bigger and brighter sky.

My hopes never come true because yesterday's dream seems so blue.

The past has gone, today is here. The future is still filled with yesterday's dreams.

IT'S ALL GOOD

It's all good when things don't go right.

It's all good when you don't know day from midnight.

It's all good when life throws you a curve.

It's all good when things are not superb.

It's all good when people began to criticize you and things are too tight.

It's all good when you think all bad things only happen to you.

It's all good when your finances are low and your friends are few.

It's all good because God will see you through and it's all good.

It is all good!!

LOOK

Look and see the magnificence of God.

See His glorious works.

Look at the beauty of the skies the ocean, and the trees.

His work is truly "EXTRAORDINARY"!

It is such a joy to look and to see His wonderful creations.

The lightning dance through the skies lights popcorn.

The fourth of July is no match for it.

The skies blazes like a fire.

It almost takes your breath away.

Who can match a man like Him?

THE DEVIL IS KNOCKING

I'm so angry at today's world until I decided to get up and do something about it. When the devil knocks at your door it is time to take a stand. I was at home minding my own business when the enemy came. I think it is wrong for people to try to make their son or daughter be a part of something they don't want. We as black people should stop being like a crab trying to pull someone else down with you. If you sell drugs don't include others. If you smoke crack keep from others and stay to yourself. Don't spread your stupidity with others. I don't want to see you trying to sell your goods to someone else. Stop being a loser and do something positive. Pull your own pants up and go to work. Stop hindering others. Stop your killing. Leave your guns home and use your power by being a mature useful citizen.

Enough is enough.

CRACK COCAINE

Crack ain't what it's all cracked up to be.

Crack is a deadly killer and it sure ain't no thriller.

Crack ain't what it's all cracked up to be.

Crack is an ugly substance it doesn't care who it robs your daddy, mama, your church, or even your job. It takes your brain and twists it around. No one can reach you unless you want to be found. You don't have one care just one blank stare searching the ground, your friends' car anywhere for the white stuff that kills, and that is real.

Crack ain't what it cracked up to be.

Your mind is too wacked, crack is trying to stick closer than glue. Finally one day you want to change then you may say oh my God I'm so ashamed.

Crack ain't what it cracked up to be.

Your heart is hurting your family is too no one knows what to do. Then you look around with one great smile it's your Lord and Savior, saying come unto me. Because you are my child. He takes you in His arms and rock you to sleep. He says rest my child you belong to me.

Crack can't win if you give the Lord a try. The future is yours if you cry unto Him. The pain is gone you can come back home.

Crack ain't what it cracked up to be.

GO AWAY CRACK COCAINE

Get back crack and go away

Jesus Word is here to stay.

Tell that ugly killer it must flee.

God is able to set you free. With Him, there is no fee.

God is good and He wants your life to be clean and if anyone can do it He can.

Rich, poor, beggar or not, God has the answer right on the spot.

There is no doubt, there's no guessing, crack has to go it can't stay run to God I believe God as I pray.

(Prayer) eavenly Father forgive me for my sins. Set me free

Save my soul and fill me with the Holy Ghost

In Jesus Name I pray

THE JAIL CELL AIN'T FOR YOU

You can't go there it ain't for you.

You can't go there you have God's work to do.

You don't have time to be locked in chains.

You have to get ready to have an abundant life because life is no game.

Get ready don't sweat, be good and faithful to God you'll have nothing to regret.

The pain of a cell will make you yell.

Give God a try then you won't have to sigh.

FREEDOM

You say us is free but I can't tell.

You still hate me. You say us is free.

I can tell you don't want to be me.

Stood by the corner in the dark last night.

You came shook me down oh, what fight.

You say I's free, me chilling outside mining

my own business you come along holling you ain't

fitting. But I's free. At least that what you told me.

But I can't tell.

MY BLACK BOYS

Yes, I have black Boys. I'm so darn glad about it.

You don't know how good it is to have them.

You can't touch that. You can't take what God gave to me.

We went through Hell and high water but that's ok we are still here.

My black boys are my black boys. I will not give them up for anything.

Smiles are all over my face when I see them.

My….. black…. boys

HE WAS ON HIS WAY

He was on his way to church. He walked past going about his business walking to church. Mind you now I said walking to church. He didn't have drugs nor did he have stolen goods. I watched and said I bet this won't be on TV. I wonder can we show some more success stories. Maybe it will help to change the world. Why don't we have a national encouragement day or is that's too much to ask for one month. I thought it was a beautiful thing to see a black man walking to church carrying a bible. Maybe that was you, but in case it wasn't start walking toward something good. TV is watching all the bad and many people are eating it up. The thing is I wonder why nobody shows some of the good things that we do while we yet live. Just know he was on his way to church, not jail.

A SEED OF HOPE

I plant a seed of hope in your life.

Filled with love instead of strife.

With this seed, I water it with the Word of God.

He will call you son and daughter.

I plant this seed as it grows hope in you and you will prosper.

God will give you His great gospel.

Without hope, you can't see things.

He does so readily for you and me.

Hope makes a poor man smile. Because he knows that he's God's child.

Hope makes a widower say I can make it even though she's hurt and can't take it.

Hope gives a man determination to feed his family even when he is tired.

A seed of hope makes you say life is worth living. Keep on going because it hopes you receiving.

I'M JUST RESTING

I'm just resting in His arms.

What do you get out of this? Are you upset?

Are you angry? No, my sis, no, my brother. I'm just resting in His

arms. Just like the springtime so beautiful and fair. I'm resting in Him.

MY HEART IS BROKEN

My heart is broken, it is filled with pain. I love my people. They don't care. They keep staying in their way. Lookout! Lookout! Here I come, but no one looks for me. Now here I am. They don't want to see me. They don't want to feel me. None are seeing the best story ever told. They pass me by while I am deep in my thoughts. It's so hard to capture their hearts, but they don't seek me, they seek their gods. That is why the night is coming soon.

RISE AND WAKE UP

In today's world, we are too busy being asleep.

We have no power we have no real motivation to be a soldier in God's army. We do not regard the coming of the soon coming king. We have been sitting in amazement at others while the pressure of life sweeps us into a daze. We must begin with the awesome powers of the living Christ the greater of the universe.

We must get back to the basics. We must enter into a deep relationship with Christ. Our goals for the new year should be already in action. We should already be fighting for the cause of Christ. We should keep a familiar song in our hearts as the universe tries to keep us in its captivity. Our main goal should be more like Christ our Divine Savior. Too often we make our own life miserable by sitting on the side.

Rise and Wake Up!!

YOU'VE GOT IT GOING ON

You've got style.

You are awesome

You have class

I've got style

You can make it

You can do it

"Encourage yourself"

Don't let life beat you down

Stand!

YOU HAVE PLUCKED ME OUT OF MY WORLD

Every day, I face many difficulties. Some come from nowhere. My heart is sometimes heavy, but I know that someway and somehow I will make it. My surroundings seem unbearable it seems that there is no hope. You came along one day and plucked me out of my world.

My world that seemed like it was crushing at something worst. It was a world of torment. But when you plucked me out of my world I knew that life could be worst, and my world was not so bad after all. Why did you pluck me out of my world?

WE ALL WANT WHAT WE WANT

Whatever we want we want it.

We don't want to wait, we are ready now.

No one wants to wait, everyone wants a quick fix plan.

When we don't get what we want we pout and we cry until we get what we want.

When things don't come to the surface immediately we have an attitude. We are totally upset.

We are strange creatures.

We can't wait so we make the wheels turn ourselves.

We are self-sufficient

We are self-made people.

We want it NOW!!

Now Now Now!!

What we Want.

Can I have my way?

If I don't I'll be mad with you.

I want to do what I want to do.

I don't care what you think.

I'm all that and a bag of chips.

THE NIGHT IS COMING

The night is coming the day is over.

There's no one looking out the window expecting me.

I'm around the corner peeping at the people as they pass by.

Their eyes are full of daze, they have no path.

WAKE UP AND SMELL THE COFFEE

Throughout the years we have heard the statement wake up and smell the coffee,

but have you thought about it? Ah-ha!! Surprisingly enough we use this

phrase to get our point across but do they get the message? Well, hope that you will

take a listen when I'm talking to you. Often we are so set in our ways and or

thoughts until we don't want to hear from anyone. We feel as though we have it

all together. Sadly enough if we would take time to smell the coffee we will see

that sometimes we have the wrong blend for our taste. We need to switch it up.

Wake Up and Smell the Coffee.

AWAKE

Awake but asleep. I gazed with the image of your face. I saw you standing with such reassurance of your beauty.

I fell in love all over again with you Lord. My mind was amazed as I stand aimlessly at the effect you have on me.

You are my inspiration, my peace, and my dreams. You are my hope for tomorrow. You and you alone can awake me out of this dreamless sleep.

To awake in the beauty of you Lord can only make me appreciate how splendid you are. My letter is to you. It has my handprint but it has been signed by your precious blood.

When I fell asleep you awake me. Therefore I shall remain awake in a sleeping world.

WE MUST DREAM THE IMPOSSIBLE

Impossible dreamers, we must take and stand. We must write our

dreams down and watch them appear before our face.

Put your best faith forward. Your desire can come true. Be inspired by keeping

your faith up high and say I can because God says I can put your best faith forward.

CALM AT SPRINGTIME

I'm calm as springtime I feel the excitement of
tomorrow. There is no worry of what may happen.
I'm just resting in His arms. I have no fear I have no doubt.

COME AND SEE A MAN

Come and see a man who knows all about me. Come and see a man who can fix any situation. He can give you everything you want. He can make you stand tall when others condemn you. He can give you a dream that will never die. He can make, the wrong right. He can restore the dead to life. He can turn midnight into bright sunshine. He can speak and make the earth tremble. He knew the future before it was earth. He can turn a beast into a beauty. He can turn that which is unwanted into something wonderfully beautiful. He can make the crooked straight. He can make the blind see. Come see a man that loves you and me. He can take a nobody and make somebody. He can turn the bad into good. He can destroy or build. He can and will bring you out.

Just come see and believe in a man that can do all things.

MEDIOCRITY

The enemy wants us to be complacent. Do something out of your routine. Many are comfortable out in the wilderness for years. Be stronger in your anointing, sow an extraordinary seed, an uncommon seed into your gift. Stretch to your next level.

WHAT HAPPEN TO YOUR DREAM

When will the day come where you will make your dreams come true. We all have the answers but when will our success come true. We are always planning to make it happen. We have all the answers but where are our answers. We will have great ideas but will we ever put them into focus?

How can we put it all together? In the meantime, our ideas and creations go unnoticed and are unsuccessful because we will never complete our dreams. I must admit me too. I have been there and done that. We won't focus long enough to complete our goals. We may feel that one day we will write a book or be a fashion model. But as time passes we will still have those same dreams wrapped up neatly in the depth of our hearts to sit idle forever. No success and of course no story. Why can't we make up our mind to work on the things that God have put in our hearts to make them a dream come true?

We find ourselves with so many things that we kept inside us and we never get off of the first base. So how can we get to the home plate? Start and stop mentally loose interest. Stop the madness, get up and make your dreams come true!

I'VE GOT A MOUNTAIN TO CLIMB

I've got a mountain to climb and it may seem small.

I've got a mountain to climb and I hope I don't fall.

I've got a mountain to climb and I guess it's just for me.

I've got a mountain to climb and I shall continue to climb until I get the victory

GO FOR THE THINGS YOU KNOW

Sometimes in life, we will not give all we have to a situation because we are afraid. We may quit in the middle of a project because of others.

We give up because we feel we don't have the knowledge to do things. We feel that everyone else can do something good. But we don't have the potential to do a thing.

Go for the things you know. We hope for things in our hearts but we won't get up and try to accomplish what we want. Let's wake up and smell the coffee. We can do whatever we set out to do. Lets, go! Lets, get involved. Lets, make it happen

Go for what you know.

DO NOT BE FORCED TO GIVE UP ON YOUR DREAMS

Day by day I think to myself how could I make it happen for me?

I think what could I do to make my dreams come true? I wonder in my mind what steps should I take to make it happen? Sitting alone watching others fulfilled their potential dreams. Makes me realize that I can do it too. There is no reason that I can't reach my goals. I must start today and focus on them and get it done. When you know that greatness is in you, you must get busy using your gifts and talents. It could make you wealthy. I have to get busy and get into practice by making my dreams come true. I must be real about doing my thing. I have to work hard at it starting now. I can't put it off for tomorrow.

Tomorrow is not promised

FOLLOW YOUR DREAM

Don't wait until it is too late to follow your dreams. Get busy and start working on your dreams. We have dreams to share, we all have something to contribute to society. Give something back to the world. Don't be afraid to launch out into the deep to discover your dreams. The sky is the limit to what you can have. Dreams are made to be accomplished work to see it become a reality. The more you think and act the quicker you can start and finish your dreams.

FREE TO BE ME

Am I really free to be me? Am I free to express myself openly? Am I free to feel and think the way I want to think? Am I wasting my time? Will I ever achieve the things I want to achieve? Am I expecting too much of myself or it is too little? Can society accept me for who I am? Or better yet do I know who I am? Can "BLACK" women really be free? Can she breathe the sweet aroma of life? Will she get better or will she get bitter? Do you think that our lives are filled with too many demands? Are the pressures of life too great?

Am I free to be me?

WHAT DO YOU HAVE TO SAY

Turn your negative into a positive. If your life gives you a lemon make lemonade. Strive for success. Don't stop and say I can't make it. Believe that you can make it happen. Stay focused and the things you want will happen. Feel free to ask God, He will bring you through.

I CAN'T SETTLE FOR LESS

I was sitting, watching, wondering, and waiting, to see what will I "REALLY" do. I wanted to know what would I say. Then the time had come it was time to put up or shut up. Life sometimes seemed unfair or downright hard. It seemed as though there was more to offer the world than what I gave. But yet, it stayed all bottled up inside, what good is that? Who would know or who could relate. Better yet who would care or even understand? Somehow I knew many would care, they would even understand. Guess what? I believe that many seem to feel that some way. Then I realize they can relate. What is she talking about? Doing things that you know you are capable of making a difference in someone else life.

JUST BEING MORE THAN YOU THINK YOU CAN BE

I'm speaking of setting out to prove to yourself that you can do something useful. Providing that you have something to say. If you give yourself a chance to just try you will see that you have many gifts and talents. Bringing it out is the problem. Doing something about it is another problem. Someone has to stir you up just to make your dreams come true. While I was writing this gift to you, the rain came. I was sitting at a beautiful riverfront with my mind filled with things to put on this page. The interpretation came to me. But I kept my mind free and stirred up with good surprise in my mind. I knew there was no stopping me now. My hand was too slow for my brain to record the thoughts that I have just for you. Our God is so filled with surprises, that we can not contain them all. We don't have a clue as to how many great gifts and surprises he has for us. He can get our hearts and minds stirred in a direction we never even thought of. How glamorous, and wonderful He is. We must keep our minds on Him.

I SAW THE MOON

I saw the moon round and full.

It looked so pretty I thought it was a pearl.

I saw the moon silvery in color.

I said to myself somewhere up there is my mother.

I stared so hard until my heart seem to split.

I saw the moon deep in sleep with my curtains cracked.

I can't get any sleep I peeped at the moon.

GET TO THE ROOT

If I had a problem I'd dig to the root. I would ask what's the problem? What's the root? The thing that hinders your spiritual life, physical life, and your finances. If you want to get to the root find out why you can't get past certain hurdles? Hurdles will bring you down. Hurdles can be conquered if you choose to go forth. This is our decision. We have no reason to fail. Jesus is on our side. He will bring us out. We can lean and depend on Him. He wants to help us, care for us, love us, and protect us. He doesn't want us to fail. He will hold you up with His hands. His hand can't fail. His hand won't fail. He won't miss.

If we listen He will be there to answer.

JESUS THE HEALER

This is about Jesus and how he heals the backslider. Jesus said return unto me my children and I will heal your backsliding. He has rebelled, committed adultery, prostitution, and defiled the earth against the Lord. There are many forms of healing pain, broken hearts, spiritual, emotional healing as well as physical healing and God can and will heal them all. Jesus said return unto me and I will heal your backsliding. He will no longer frown on us, but he would be merciful to us. We may lie down in the shame and disgrace that covers us. But know that we must repent to be healed.

CHRISTMAS EVE

Christmas eve is filled with excitement, love, and peace. Hearts are filled with joy and great expectations. Everyone is waiting for time to pass by hoping that they could take a peep in their packages. No matter how large or small we all wait for a gift or some token of appreciation. Some people are disappointed some people receive no gifts. Some have no gift to give. Some people want to be loved. Some people want to give love. No matter what situation we all await Christmas eve because we know that soon it will be Christmas.

Have a very joyous Christmas!

LITTLE PEOPLE

Waiting in the delight of Christmas. Their eyes are glittering with the expectation of toys and all sorts of goodies. They want to have a good Christmas they want to experience love and all of God's good blessings. Every tear dried on Christmas day. Nothing but smiles. Because God did visit their house. He put wealth in their stocking. He put health in their stockings. He put love in their stockings. He came and gave all He had He gave His life. And best of all He "Rose" from the dead. He appeared to His people. He is a wonderful and miraculous gift. He gave us life and life more abundantly.

THE SEASON IS RIGHT

This is the time of the year when love should be ringing in the air. Peace should be smelling out like a gentle rose. This is the time and season when all of us should clap our hands together in unity. We all should be thinking of one thing...."Others". We should have the spirit of love, contentment, restoration, and undying faith. We should give the greatest gift that we could ever give and that is our very own life. If we surrender our total life and heart to Him, we will give Him the greatest gift we could ever give. Eternal life is what we should want. It makes sense to live forever in peace and not condemnation. His peace He gives to you.

He died so we might live.

SOON AND VERY SOON

Soon and very soon our creator of this universe will be coming back. There will be no more trying to get real with God. It will be all over. We can't say wait give me another chance for us to get caught up in the air with Him. How wonderful it will be to be caught up in the air with the Savior. All our problems and fears will be gone forever. No more stress, sickness, death, and no more diseases. There will be peace forevermore. Who could stand the test of being left here alone without Christ in your life? My heart is filled with excitement for our new resurrected bodies. How could we ever make it on this earth without our awesome God?

TODAY IS A NEW BEGINNING

Today is the beginning of a new dawn. Today is a time to be victorious in the middle of a storm. Today is a day to express your fears. Let's sit and watch God make them disappear. Today is the beginning of a new creation. Today is the time for new hope and a new nation. How great it is to wake up with the freedom to cry out and worship the Lord. He is our armor as well as our sword. Today is a new beginning for all our dreams, hopes, and desires to be fulfilled. Today is a new beginning for me to tell you the creator of this universe is truthful and He is real.

GET UP AND GET WITH THE REAL WORLD

We will only be what we want to be. We will accomplish only what we think we can accomplish. We sometimes feel inferior to others when they are just like us struggling to survive. Many are just as miserable. We stand back and pass judgment on others but we are in just as much of a fix as they are. We look out at our life through rose-colored glasses. We think we have no stains. We need to get up and get with the real world.

LORD IT IS SO PRETTY

Lord, I like how pretty the music sound to my ears. I like how all the instruments come together and make a lovely melody. Why can't man get together and have a melody of sweet music that is so good to hear? Why can't men's lives be more pretty? I like the sun, how pretty it is. It has the color of burnt orange. Lord, it is so pretty. I love the fragrance of flowers as I hold them in my hands they are so pretty, I like when the Lord makes the due drops fall on the roses. It all seems so special to me.

I like that Lord it is so pretty.

TIME IS NO ESSENCE

Time is no essence to God. Time has no end. Time is just another way of getting by with what I should do but didn't do. We use time as an excuse to be disobedient to God's calling on our life. We say it's not enough time. We say it's not enough time. We feel that we shouldn't go out of our way for others.

HOME

He's gone home. He is never alone. He gave one look. There was not another breath he took. He left in a flash, no one knew of the great big dash. He stood tall ready to meet the Lord. No problem as God gently called. God had a master plan. He said this is a great and humble man. Come on home

IMPERFECT PEOPLE BUT SAVED

As death crept sometimes slow and sometimes quickly, I've begun to learn some significant things about death. Even though in my mind I felt that we had to live a perfect life to make it to heaven. We may miss perfection but God can still take us home. We have lost many people in our family in the last few years. My dad lost many brothers and a sister. He lost a brother-In-law as well as his wife my mom. I can see now as I sit to listen to hear what everyone had to say, that God will help us to become perfect before we go home. He gave them just enough time to get ready to make it to heaven.

DEAR GOD

I'm so glad to know you. I'm happy that you have chosen me to serve you. I can hardly imagine my being chosen to do great works for you. I have always thought a little down on myself because I didn't think I was smart enough. God takes those nobodies and makes somebody. God, you are my life. I want to be a better person. I want you to be a part of my every moment. You give special care and concern to me. The more I know you the more I want to know you.

Dear God, It is me

ALL I NEED IS YOU

All I need is love, just like flowers need rain to live. All I need is love to hold me close each day. All I need is your warm embrace to hold my hand as I continue on this journey. All I need is you, you are the one who cares. Your love doesn't fail all I need you, Lord.

HE CAME THROUGH

Once again He came through for us. We must come together to worship him. He has richly blessed us. He knows our every need. He doesn't mind seeing about His children. He will make away out of no way. You think you are alone but He never leaves you alone.

GIVE

Give an everlasting gift that will not wither nor will it fade. Give a helping hand to the downtrodden. Give to the ones who backslid from Christ. Give them the sweet undisputed word of God. Give more than you receive. Give them Hope. Give them "JESUS".

LEAN ON GOD AND YOU WON'T GO WRONG.

If you lean on God you can't go wrong. Leaning on God should come naturally but we sometimes get caught in our own ways and say we can fix it. We say we can make the wheels turn. But there's no way we can make any wheel turn. We only wish that we could. Lean on God and you won't go wrong. You will see the bad turn into good. You will see the negative turn into a positive. You will witness the sick to be healed. You will see the imprisoned set free. The darkness will become light. As we strive each day we will become stronger with each step. God is great and He is our creator. He will make the crooked road straight.

SHOW THE STORM OF YOUR LOVE LORD

Let only the storm of love come. Show us your magnificent beauty. Let the world grasp for breath as the earth stands silent. Let the pain of suffering be no more. Let the trees blow the scent of your fragrance in our nostrils. Let your beauty be beyond our comprehension. Let our eyes be in amazement of your ecstasy. Let the rich say that I am poor. Let the poor say that I am rich. Let your storm be a storm of your love, power and let your embrace forever be in our hearts. Let the heavens bow down before you and let the earth say I am glad. Let our souls rejoice and reign in you, because of your precious love. Let our storm be centered by the eye of your love.

PRECIOUS

Precious is the one who died for me. Precious is the one who hung on a tree for me.

Precious is He that was pierced in His side for me.

Precious is He that locked his head between His shoulders and sighed.

Precious is He who never gave up. Precious is He who sat at the last supper and supped.

Precious is God who gave His Son.

Precious is He who knew the world would need a redeemer for everyone.

Precious is the Savior who gave, so I might live. His deep and precious love would always freely give.

Perhaps one day He will come back like a sonic boom.

We will feel His precious love more than we can merely consume.

He gave His life so that I could live twice.

A PEACE OF MIND

I just want peace of mind. I don't need anger or strife of any kind. In the midst of a storm, I called your name. It didn't take very long, and you gently came. My heart was overcome with fear and doubt. You whispered one word and everything worked out. All I wanted was peace of mind. You came along and said, to me, you will have peace.

FOUNTAIN OF YOUTH

The fountain of youth was a myth that everyone remembers.

They say they like to see it but what can you do if it doesn't happen to you.

Will you still dream of a fountain of youth?

Your face shows wrinkles your mind is forgetting.

My secret that I never told is how I fear the day of growing old.

Teardrops come streaming down my cheek. Afraid of reality scared of growing weak.

SILENT

*Silent tears in the night, cold and lifeless in my sight. Many are
asleep but I'm awake as I sit peacefully awaiting the sun to
break. I can't believe how I sit and cried just watching and
waiting for time to fly. If someone asks what's wrong with me
I'll say nothing is the matter and then I'll get sadder. Silent was
I and I didn't say a word. Oh, what a night I couldn't even hear
a bird. All hope was gone or so it seem.*

*Then I saw a smiling face with eyes full of gleam. Who could it
be I patiently asked? No one knew as I took a quick glance. He's
so beautiful I couldn't even phantom. Even His presence made
me shatter. It was the light from heaven. It was God and His
whole team. Silent was they with outstretched hands talking to
me as they say we are your favorite fans. We cheered you on
when you were down. We gave you hope when you felt like a
clown. We gave you a boost when you were all choked up inside.
We helped you to get here and make it with dignity. Silent,
silent, in the night, as you come home to your God who cares
and whose love you often share.*

FADED BEAUTY

Faded is the beauty of my old wrinkled face. No one sees in my heart how it drips with pain and disgrace.

Faded is the beauty of this old body my eyes are growing dim and I'm not the life of the party anymore.

I use to be hipped and all in style but now look at me I'm back to being a little child.

Tears are in my eyes my hands are racked with pain. Oh, that old beauty it didn't remain. I want to give up and want to quit. But then I heard a voice from heaven saying hang on in there you can't stop and sit idle.

Faded beauty I thought it was over but God came to give that precious inner beauty that will never disappear. Just open your heart and you will certainly hear.

Faded beauty enters into my rest. When I touch you, you can't help but be beautiful and deeply blessed. You are a star and you have a crown. God's grace and His word can never let you down.

Faded Beauty come on Home

PRAYER

Lord help us to know you. Help us to praise you. Give us the strength to go on. Let us remember why you went on the Calvary cross. Make us holy. Make us new. Create in us a new beginning give us HOPE for tomorrow. Give us grace for today. Make our lives be the joy that surrounded the earth. Let hard trails be turned into gladness.

Let our pain not be in vain.

THE LAST RACE

Sitting waiting on time that seems to tick slowly, I wonder how it will be when God gets ready for us. Will we be ready for the race or will we stop in the middle and say I can't make it? Will we say it's not worth it? With all of my heart and my being, I want us to make it to the end. The end will come and our minds will race with the excitement of the coming King. Our hope and determination are to win. The last race is coming can you make it through the last hurdle? Sweat may be popping but you can make it through the last race. Our heart is raining with excitement about being in the last race. There's no fear because our eyes are steady and our minds are on Jesus.

I'M DRUNK WITH THE DREAMS

I'm Drunken with the dreams that should have already come into existence. Why am I not getting to the care of my destiny? So much is wrapped up in my mind. So many dreams that I dare not let pass me by. There is always the hope that my dreams will come to reality. Therefore I shall not stop now. I can't afford to give up now. There is so much bottled up inside of this heart that I can only share with my God. I mustn't tell a soul, less they laugh me to scorn. Who does she think she is? What makes her all that? So I stay drunk with my dreams.

GET UP AND WIN

Too often we start and never finish. We want to make it. But never enter the race. Be like Paul he said "I have fought a good fight, I have finished my course, I have kept the faith". 2 Timothy 4:7 Get up and begin by giving God your heart. Nothing can keep you from receiving your just reward on that glorious day. Not even the principalities of darkness. Keep your eyes on the real prize, Jesus Christ. We may work on a job all of our lives and still lose. What does it profit a man to gain the whole world and lose his soul? Quitters never win and winners never quit.

DAYTONA

We are taking this land back. We will trample over the forces of darkness. We will scream out loud "WE TAKE BACK DAYTONA".

We take back our neighborhood

We take back our children

We take back our men

We take back our freedom

We take back what is rightfully ours.

We will take "BACK OUR LAND"

We will not sit back and let the devil take the people to the pit of hell. We will claim our victory through Jesus Christ!

THE STRONG IS COMING FORTH

The cries of the strong are being heard. Our voices will ring out loudly. We will sing out the melody of Jesus Christ. Our only survival is through His mighty strong hands. Our cry to Him will save us. Our believing in Him will make us strong. Our testimonies will stand. Our survival is only because He is strong. He is our strength. He is our refuge. On Him will we depend on. Strong is having our inner being renewed and made whole. But they that wait upon the Lord shall renew their strength; they shall mount up with wings as eagles; they shall run, and not be weary, and they shall walk, and not faint. Isaiah 40:31

DRIFTING

Watching the smoothness of the ocean waves, I sit back to relax and observe the serenity of another world I have not yet seen.

The motors of the ship roar to the success of our glorious arrival.

All so peaceful and full of hope. We sit back and listen with great expectation.

Respecting each other's privacy we silently wait for our destination.

Anxious to see this uncrown world.

We hold on to our excitement, our faces are full of anticipation.

The almost sad ending of this cruise is drawing nigh.

We have not yet grasped the wonderful hospitality we've yet to receive.

Too often we have forgotten our blessings.

Nevertheless, we sail into a beautiful world that God has created.

My eyes can not believe nor my mind can comprehend the beauty of just the sail.

I'm looking for miracles yet expecting nothing.

How excellent it is for God to have allowed this day to appear.

He gives us freedom as well as wealth.

Oh, how excellent is His wonderful name.

How overwhelming it is to feel his charming presence at this very moment as I sit and write these most magnificent words.

There's no greater feeling than right now. I write I read because it makes me happy. It's a sense of belonging and a feeling of beauty.

It allows me to express myself and to be myself.

Not an imitation of me but a real me. Too many times I've let the world express to me what I should be, never letting the Lord do the creating and reshaping me. Now I'm more into pleasing God rather than man. I always wonder what does man thinks of me. What a terrible thought. What an awful life you work yourself into stress just to please man. What about God? Never enough time for Him. Always in a hurry, hurry, rush, rush, rush. Never slow down and take it easy. Time is short, but so is life. This is me this is who I am, this is the natural and awesome one who God put His seal of approval on. Why can't we all accept each other including me?

Written on a cruise to Nassau Bahamas

SOLD OUT

What are we sold out to? Are we as a nation sold out? Are we as a person sold out to what people say? Are you sold out as lawyers to not speak out for our black brothers and sisters? As a mom are we sold out? As a dad are you sold out? Are we sold out to keep our mouths shut because "Massa" might get us? Has fear kept our mouths shut down? Our mouths are closed tight because of the fear of our consequences. We fear the unknown, we fear what can happen to us. Suppose you lose your job? Or the police get mad and hurt you because you spoke out. Now you wondering what's going to happen to your family? It's so many reasons why we don't speak up and speak out. We know what is right but because of the fear of the unknown, we stay silent. We let each other sink in the sand when we could save each other. I say we because me just like you say I've got my kids out there and if I don't speak out someone will hurt them.

Why the heck they are being knocked around anyway. They are being abused, beaten why? So why not talk about it? It's my turn now. They go to jail just like your people. We feel the pain of being locked up and beat up.

We have black-on-black crime. We have police brutality. We have domestic abuse by our own locked up minds. We can't get out of one thing before another thing comes to our front door. The ones who suppose to protect us are worst than the crime makers. We are all sold out to something. We can't focus because of fear, terror, and the shame of life problems. Therefore we began to slowly meltdown because we can't stand the pressures of life. We become weak just like our ancestors whipped to the core. They came over in boats, only to get our people locked in jail cells like sardines in a can and we accept it. We have become comfortable with it. We don't fight for our freedom. We have to grin and bear it. The judges know but what do they do. The judge appeases the officials by saying guilty without really looking into the whole matter. They pack it up and say the court is adjourned. When it's really not adjourned. We go home with our tails tucked between our legs waiting for a phone call to come from our loved ones.

Billy Bob and the judge go out to lunch and discuss the next case spending money, money. The lawyers get fat with new hard-earned money in their pockets, as they wait for their next case. In the mean time I'm pissed off. I'm mad with the whole world because I can't get anyone to hear my plead.

So who sold out to our families. Our families suffer because I'm too afraid of what the people say. I'm sold out to God. We must let God see us through all of these crazy trails. I say that my daughters are in jail because God needs them. That is the only reason they are in there. I feel it in my spirit. God is on time. He can make the crooked road straight. We are ready for our job to be completed. We will help others go through these light afflictions. It doesn't matter what we go through it is a reason for it. We must stand up and go on. We must finish the course, we must finish with faith. We must get on board to save a dying world. I'm must because the courts didn't hear us. They heard who they wanted to hear. There are reasons why things go the way they do. I don't see why people are not trained to help the mentally challenged.

But I know God sits high and looks low. He will still get the glory. Be patient and watch God makes miracles happen in your situation. God loves us and He makes the bad turn to good.

www.ingramcontent.com/pod-product-compliance
Lightning Source LLC
Chambersburg PA
CBHW070752180626
46818CB00007B/3090